Synopsis of a Grave

Navya Navely

Dedication

To my sister,

For her unwavering support and blind trust in all that I did.

To my grandparents, and parents,

for their love and nourishment that made me capable enough to believe in myself.

And to the people who broke my heart, who inspired me to start writing poetry.

Thank You.

Foreword

In this exceptional collection of poems, the author invites us to a rather semi-dystopian world, where all barriers of communication cease to exist, and words paint a psychedelic picture for us to dive into.

The english language becomes a canvas for emotion, thought, and introspection.

With a lyrical grace and a keen eye for detail, the author explores themes of love, heartbreak, yearning, and detachment, weaving together moments of beauty and contemplation.

I

Your face turns blurry,
As I close my eyes in an attempt to live an untrue
dream.
Don't wake me up, this dream is precious.
Although it may be a figment of my imagination...
It is my only regime.

Don't wake me up,
Don't hurt yourself for me the way you did back then.
Don't return my love, don't act alright or pretend.
Don't break your already fragmented heart,
Acting as if I can't comprehend.

The scars you once helped me heal, now yearn for your
touch.
The letters you long ago gave me, near my heart I
clutch.
As I wail until there are no more tears left to cry.
Remembering the nights, we talked so much there was
nothing left to pry. As I sit here, pondering how hard it
will be to bid our last goodbye.

Your picture gets blurrier, while the dream comes to an
end.
I slowly start to forget myself but cross my heart and
hope to die,
Aim the needle in my eye.
I'll always remember you but only with a sigh.

2

You were a laugh in the sea of sadness.
My melancholic heart and blunt scars you once
caressed...
Are now filled with your abundant cries.
A knife in my hand, with blood dripping down my wrist
and thighs...
How could I be so dense?
Your happy giggles were indeed only a disguise.

The hiraeth your quiescent soul felt,
Must've been so agonising, I wish I could take it all.
The darkness your lonely eyes held...
Must've been so excruciating, for you to take that fall.

The morning after you left,
I woke up with a different shade of blue.
A miserable one, where my eyes couldn't even turn to
look at you.
And I couldn't, even if I wanted to...
Because you were no longer there.
I could see your arms, your torso, your legs,
Your eyes that no longer held any movement,
I just couldn't see you.

3

I can still taste the ash on my tongue,
From the last time you burnt me with your kiss.
You grew lovesome flowers within my lungs,
But they only make my heart feel more abyss.

And each cut left on my skin by your touch,
Bleeds out in the winter, staining the snow
crimson.
As my quivering voice pleas to not be adjudged,
You edge your knife towards my throat with
dominion.

And now as my eyes shed tears of blood,
You smile from a distance and say, "Agony is
real beauty".
But your actions state that I'm still not loved...
Even when all I'm made of is fragmented pieces
of misery.

4

My heart craves for more of your lies,
With blue clouds thundering above, full of
woe.
Love slips away from in between my fingers,
breaking ties...
As I realise, time isn't a glance away anymore.

You were a canvas painted on a Tuesday night
With blood, tears and sweat.
Though it seemed as if haunting pleas in
plight,
Rather more of a comfort through your gentle
silhouette.

The flame inside me burns for your wishes
That long to be a part of reality.
You draped a blanket of melancholy over me,
And though I'm warm, I burn with agony.

5

You looked at me like I was a
masterpiece,
But you weren't interested in art.
You provided me with comfortable
agony,
But now my life is blood bath.

As I watch myself from afar,
My blood filled life slipping away from
me.
Coming across joy in the process…
The tears on my grave play me a
symphony.

Now I lie there still…
My quiescent mind running parallel to
rue;
A familiar music plays in distance,
As I wail, while the colours of music
paint me blue.

It's become a habit to bite the silver hand that feeds
me.
It seems, I've done everything wrong.
The hands soft, supple, satisfying but not
anymore…
They used to provide me with love and comfort,
But are now full of woe.
Expectations, so many of them, for me so much.
They overflow my jar of misery, so i desire to
disappoint.
I do not have an appetite for another expectance,
So I'll bite to bleed this time.
The blood turns green and flows down the street,
Writing a death note as it leaves.
I'll feed on it like a vampire and I'll lick the overflow
I'll scratch my eyes raw,
And puke the blood out of overdose.
I'll embrace the inhumane underneath me,
And inhale the blue smoke.
It's time for something in me to die
To bring me back anew
So, I beg the crow on the doug fir tree,
To pick on my eyes built of rue.

7

And oh God,
Why shall you provide me with eyes,
If I can't capture mother nature's beauty?
Why shall I be given the privilege to speak,
If I can't find the right words to console my
lover?
Why shall I receive the blessing of hearing,
If I can't listen to my mother's cries?
Oh God,
Why shall I be the one who's blessed
And not the one who deserves the kindness
of man who's blessed?

8

I've carried the ghost of my past for too
long,
And I'm haunted by those who are still
alive.
I bleed myself dry in a reality beyond,
As the corpse of autumn stabs me in plight.

The spilled truth on my shirt crawls its way
Towards my tongue, and it only get bitter.
It paints my tongue blue,
And laughs at me for my fidelity to failure.
It makes my teeth weak,
And follows the path to my heart,
Only to play a dead beat.
It holds my head under water,
It smashes my head on the concrete.

But as the cycle of destruction goes on
I realise it wasn't the truth
That was planning these atrocities…
All along, it was only me.

9

You played a symphony from the broken
pieces of my heart,
And though it's melodious, it makes my ears
bleed through.
All my self inflicted pain is a memoir to myself
from the past,
Whom I've buried in a graveyard so blue.

My drought and flood coexist underneath my
grave,
As I lie there waiting for my funeral to be held.
The misery you painted me with lies to my
face,
When I ask about our hearts that once
rebelled.

The reality who is friends with my grief,
Has now learned to mock me.
It follows me around… manipulating my every
belief,
And my only escape left is fantasy.

IO

You bathe me in a pool of misery,
And you are the pigment of my sorrows.
You bleed my heart dry 'til it's weary,
And drain my mind hollow.

When October arrived with a loud entrance,
Its silence triggering my chaos.
A rope in its hand, a threat to end it...
And put everything to a pause.

That's when you returned, in the middle of my
path,
Taken aback with your destruction that
painted the world red...
You ran yourself an ice bath,
But my blood ran cold instead.

II

Your abuse was my favourite symphony,
And it burns every time you take it away.
I still hold the ashes of my soul discreetly,
But they come back to life every time they
meet your gaze.

Everytime I face you, my mouth becomes a
graveyard of pleas,
And my chest morphs into a haunted house
left untouched.
You held my heart with such force, I could
map out every crease,
But its cries of agony are still hushed.

You warned me not to hold onto your hand,
For blades from your past battles are stuck
to it still.
The sharpness now stabs me deep,
As I bleed out staining your morals ill.

12

I hope this winter goes easy on me,
As the cold has already gotten to my
heart.
It stains the snow with your honey words
and agony,
And it gave me your tears to mould you
and me apart.

You painted an ethereal picture, with all
the vivid colours,
But you failed to realise I was colourblind.
You were the nostalgic summer,
When falling for you was my only crime.

Now that very nostalgia devours me raw,
As it paints me with smoke and smears me
with guilt.
I spit out the blood, whilst you aim for my
jaw,
And the flowers on my grave find another
reason to wilt.

13

I hope the sun rises tomorrow with a dark
shade of grey,
And the moon with a bright crimson.
May the dullness of the day scare the souls of
our inner demons away,
And quench their thirst with blood dripping
from the moon ablaze.

A beginning of an apocalypse in our galaxy,
And a fierce battle to be fought with blunt
blades.
A mist of victory, a tale of misery,
A melody of glory only wolves could taste.

Embrace the envy stuck in the past,
And walk on clouds of battles and wars.
The warmth of the embrace you gave me at my
last,
Has burnt my heart down to its last flame.

14

My knees are scraped,
and my tongue tastes like blood.
I'm on the ground in defeat,
And I'm covering my ears as their laughs
get louder.
I feel them pointing at me,
And myself slipping away.
Because, who am I,
If not the flaws my mother tried to
suppress?
Who am I, if not the spite my father spat
away?
Who am I, if not the monsters they see in
themselves everyday?

15

I fidget a lighter to ignite the cigarette
You hold between your supple lips.
The cigarette tinted red from the stain
of your lipstick.
I flick the lighter aflame,
And burn your soul instead.
Your vanilla scent frisking away,
Its presence being filled by the smell of
your smoke leading me astray.
And by the time I realise it's not your
cigarette that I set ablaze,
I think to myself,
As your soul burned in disdain.

16

I'm no writer,
But for you I'd fill the pages of your heart
with tales of our love.
I'm no artist,
But for you I'd paint the sky the colour of
your lips.
I'm no musician,
But for you I'd sing symphonies of your cries.
I'm no one without the comfort of your
embrace,
Or the taste of your lips on mine.
I'm no one without the sound of your giggle
when I tell a joke,
Or your scent that takes me back to the night
we met.
I'm no one without your lipstick stained
kisses on my face,
Or your tears that my shirt once soaked.
I'm no one without your love, your sorrow,
your soul, your hatred.
I'm no one without you.

17

To the first man I ever loved:
I beg grief to stay away from me and
you.
But when you blink,
It finds the right time.
Now that you're asleep,
It has stricken with pain.
I beg the gods of heaven to return my
beloved…
But they only respond with thunder
and rain.
I watched the sun set a particular day,
And begged the stars to let the selfless
souls that sacrificed their blood for the
sky to be stained red, rest well for
eternity.
But they only twinkled in shame.
Whom should I beg now?
Because wishes only worked when you
were here to fulfil them.

18

I'm a museum of broken pieces of glass,
For I invest my heart in losing battles.
The battlefield confides in me how many
blood-filled tears she holds.
Yet she yearns for a war to be held upon
her.
She dies for the knight and comes alive for
the divine.
Lying there in his hushed presence of light,
She resumes her preaching.
From dusk till dawn not a moment of
peace,
Wishing upon her demise,
Lies an unseen crease.
The divine power that once held her with
grace,
Has now abandoned her, to her dismay.
Now again, she lies with a sword in hand,
Confiding in another soldier, of the traitor
that is man.

19

The coral shade of the sky smelled
like the scent of your cheeks,
when you intertwined your hand
with mine.
The sun pulled the ocean for a kiss
as deep as the sky,
When you spun me in the daylight.
The waves hugged the sand as if to
never see it again,
When you embraced me with
warmth that made me ignite.
And I just know it wasn't Romeo &
Juliette or Antony & Cleopatra
that inspired them for such sights.
It was you and me, me and you.

20

She was like a shot of vodka,
At the end of a tiring day.
Yet somehow exactly like the rose she
gave me on a withering day.
She lies in the unfinished letters,
left to burn in my room;
As well as in the half burnt cigarettes
clinging onto my lips.
She sits in the withering flowers I once
gave her,
That once depicted my heart and
bloomed.
But now she stays in a corner of my
mind,
Instead of my eyes.
She swiftly moves with the wind
entering through the window,
And takes her leave with each breath I
lose.

21

If my heart must break,
Let it have your name written all over
it.
For that is the only way I could
watch you shatter.
If I must burn with love,
Burn my tongue with the fuel your
heart runs on.
For that is the only way I could taste
you.
If I must fall to oblivion,
Let me fall in your love first.
For that is the only aid that could
heal my wounds.

22

I would've given you my bones,
If you just as much as asked for wood,
To start an everyday fire.
I would've given you my soul,
If my body wasn't up to your desire.
I would've slashed my tongue,
If the gash could've housed your tongue with
comfort.
And I surely would've skinned myself alive,
If the warmth of my blood wasn't enough to
keep you for the night.
As it turns out,
The blood turned cold, brewing in your hatred
with spite.
I apologise,
I should've made room for you,
And kept my organs aside.

23

The forewarned still decided to walk
the earth,
Put an end to the dystopian hearts.
The gashes they housed,
Were once home to warmth.
And the minds that rebelled,
Were thrown off to battle the French.
And though they had learned of
Versailles,
The stolen flags of peace were waved
too soon.
The war subdued,
But left me jewels to be adorned by
you.

Author's Note

Thank you for taking the time
out of your day to read
something so dear to me.

I never once imagined my deepest
thoughts could be tolerated by
others if I put them on display.

I'm truly grateful.

Yours Sincerely,
Navya Navely

www.ingramcontent.com/pod-product-compliance
Lightning Source LLC
Chambersburg PA
CBHW031810150726
47989CB00006B/2947